W9-AOL-627

ANDERSON ELEMENTARY LIBRARY SCHOOL

A ROOKIE BIOGRAPHY

A. A. MILNE

Author of Winnie-the-Pooh

By Marlene Toby

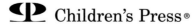
Children's Press ®

A Division of Grolier Publishing
New York London Hong Kong Sydney
Danbury, Connecticut

ANDERSON ELEMENTARY LIBRARY SCHOOL

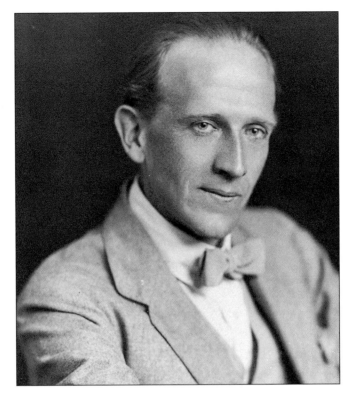

A. A. Milne 1882-1956

Library of Congress Cataloging-in-Publication Data

Toby, Marlene.
    A. A. Milne (author of *Winnie-the-Pooh*) / by Marlene Toby.
        p. cm. — (A Rookie biography)
    Includes index.
    Summary: The life of A. A. Milne, the creator of *Winnie-the-Pooh*, told in very simple language.
    ISBN 0-516-04270-X
    1. Milne, A. A. (Alan Alexander), 1882-1956—Juvenile literature 2. Authors, English—20th
Century—Biography—Juvenile literature. 3. Winnie-the-Pooh (Fictitious character)—Juvenile
literature. 4. Children's stories—Authorship—Juvenile literature. [1. Milne, A. A. (Alan Alexander),
1882-1956. 2. Authors, English.] I. Title. II. Series: Toby, Marlene. Rookie biography.
PR6025.I65Z66 1995
828 '.91209 — dc20
[B]   95-10108
                                                                                                    CIP
                                                                                                     AC

Copyright 1995 by Children's Press®, Inc.
All rights reserved. Published simultaneously in Canada.
Printed in the United States of America.

1 2 3 4 5 6 7 8 9 10 R 04 03 02 01 00 99 98 97 96 95

Alan Alexander Milne lived
from 1882 to 1956. He wrote
many books for adults. He also
wrote poems for children and
two books about a stuffed toy
bear he called Winnie-the-Pooh.
This is Mr. Milne's story.

CONTENTS

Alan Milne was born in London, England,
in 1882.

Chapter 1

The Milne Boys

Papa Milne pointed to
a word on a wall chart.
"What's that?" he asked
his sons. Barry didn't
know the word and he
was almost five. Ken
didn't know the word,
and he was almost four.

Alan was just 2 1/2 years
old. He sat in the corner
and played with his toys.

"I know it," he said. "It's cat!" Alan was right.

Alan could read before he was four and write before he was five. Papa Milne was proud of him.

Alan's father owned a small school for boys in London, England. It was called Henley House. The Milne family lived in one part of the building, and the school was in the other part.

When Alan turned six, he started school at Henley House. He liked going to school with his brother Ken. They were best friends.

Alan and Ken shared secrets and did everything together. "Together [said Alan] we had no fears of anybody or anything...."

Ken was a smart boy. However, Alan was even smarter. Whenever there was a contest, Alan always won. But that never made Ken angry.

*A hilly part of London as it might have looked
when Alan Milne was growing up*

When not in school,
Ken and Alan took
long bicycle rides and
imagined being in other
countries. Often they
walked for miles in the
country collecting rocks
and chasing butterflies.
Their dog Brownie went
everywhere with them.

Sometimes, the two
boys rolled hoops and
played rough games on
the playground. And
always, they daydreamed
about being sailors.

Westminster School, in London

Chapter 2

Let's Go Together

When Ken turned twelve, he
went to Westminster School.
A year later, Alan joined him.

Westminster was old and
famous. It had many
problems. There was no
hot water for baths. The
food tasted terrible. And
the older boys were hard
on the younger ones. Alan
didn't like those things,
but he did like learning.

Right: A classroom at Westminster. Life at Westminster School was hard. To make learning more fun, Alan and Ken made up games and secret codes.

Alan was a good student. He liked math best of all. He worked hard to advance two levels so that he could be with Ken.

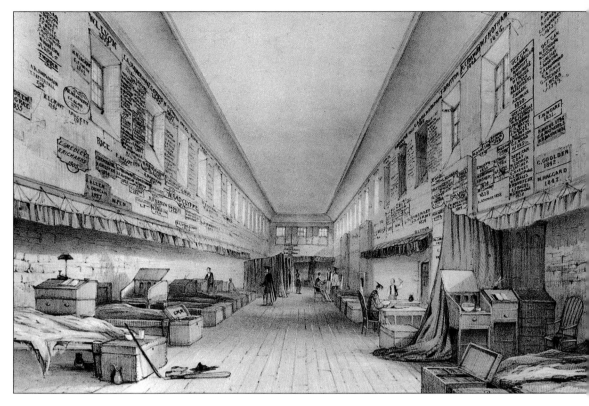

A dormitory at Westminster School where boys slept and kept their things

Ken and Alan did many things together at Westminster. They played the usual boyish games with friends. They also played against each other in cricket and soccer matches.

ANDERSON ELEMENTARY SCHOOL LIBRARY

During class they wrote
letters to each other in
secret codes. Every Sunday,
they wrote to their parents.

In 1898, Ken left
Westminster to study law.
He wrote wonderful letters
to Alan and to his parents.
Alan wrote back.

In the letters, Alan and
Ken made up funny rhymes.
They put the rhymes in the
Westminster school paper.
Everyone thought they
were funny.

In 1900, Alan left Westminster and went to Trinity College at Cambridge University. He was eighteen. He studied math but wanted to be a writer.

He started writing funny rhymes for Cambridge's magazine, *The Granta*. The rhymes were called nonsense verses. Sometimes Alan and Ken wrote verses together. They signed them "A. K. M."

Then, in 1902, Alan became editor of *The Granta*. It was a hard job, but Alan loved it. He wanted to keep writing after he graduated from Cambridge.

Trinity College Chapel at Cambridge University

Chapter 3

So Many Things to Do

Alan's father was worried
about how Alan would
make a living. He thought
that Alan might work for
the government. Alan
didn't like that idea.

Next he suggested that
Alan become a teacher.
Alan didn't like that
either. "I'd like to try
to be a writer," said Alan.

*Alan Milne had one goal in mind—to be
a writer.*

*By 1890, many young writers were trying to
make a name for themselves in London.*

Alan's father told him
how hard it was for a
writer to earn enough
money. Alan knew that.
But he still wanted to
try. So he moved into
an apartment in London
and started writing.

By the end of the first
year, Alan had sold some
stories to newspapers and
magazines. But he hadn't
made much money, and
that worried him.

The next year, Alan's first book, *Lovers in London*, came out. Then a few of his articles appeared in *Punch*, a funny London magazine.

In 1906, the editor of *Punch* asked Alan to be his assistant. Alan was twenty-four years old. He thought the job was perfect.

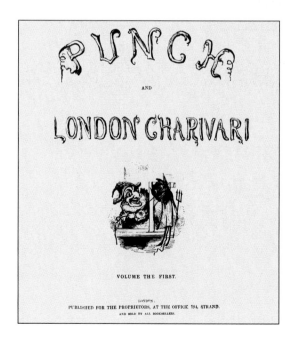

Left: The first issue of Punch *came out in 1841. Every Saturday there was a new issue.*

Opposite page: Funny characters were often put on the covers.

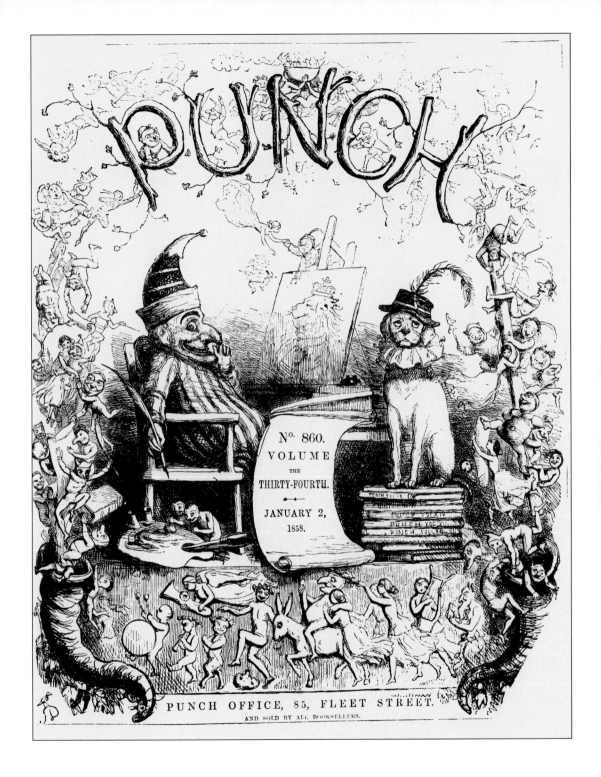

PUNCH

N°. 860.
VOLUME
THE
THIRTY-FOURTH.
JANUARY 2,
1858.

PUNCH OFFICE, 85, FLEET STREET.
AND SOLD BY ALL BOOKSELLERS.

The next years were good
ones. Ken got married.
Alan published his second
book, *The Day's Play*, and
he spent more time with
family and friends.

In 1913, Alan met Dorothy
Selincourt. He called her
"Daphne" or "Daff" and
thought that she "had the
most perfect sense of humor
in the world." In June they
married and moved into an
apartment in Chelsea.

World War I broke out in
1914. Although Alan hated
war, he joined the army as
a signals officer. As a signals
officer he thought he would
not have to kill anyone.
Still, Alan went to the
front lines in France.

As the war continued,
Daphne and other soldiers'
wives thought of ways to
entertain the troops. Alan
helped them by writing a
play. The fairy story, called
Once on a Time, was about a
prince, a princess, a wicked
countess, and a magic ring.

World War I was fought in the trenches. Alan caught trench fever in France.

When Alan caught a disease called trench fever, he was sent home. After he got well, he did not go back to his job at *Punch*. Instead, he wrote plays.

Some of his plays are *The Lucky One*, *The Boy Comes Home*, *Belinda*, *Mr. Pimm Passes By*, and *Make-Believe*.

Chapter 4

"The Best Bear in All the World"

In the summer of 1920, Daphne gave birth to a little boy. She named him Christopher Robin.

Daphne and Alan loved their little boy. He brought them a lot of joy. He also changed Alan's life as a writer.

Opposite page: Daphne Milne and Christopher Robin in 1926. Christopher was six years old.

When Christopher was
two, Alan wrote a poem
about him saying his
prayers. It was called
"Vespers."

Alan liked the poem
when it was finished.
He thought he would
like to write more
poems for children.

Opposite page: Alan Milne and Christopher Robin in 1926

The Wales countryside

When Christopher was three,
the Milnes went to Wales for
the summer. It rained almost
every day. While it rained, Alan
watched his son Christopher
play. He thought about his
own childhood, too, and how
he and Ken played. Then he
began to write.

For eleven days, Alan wrote
poems for children. One poem
he called "The Dormouse and
the Doctor."

There once was a Dormouse who lived in a bed
Of delphiniums (blue) and geraniums (red),
And all the day long he'd a wonderful view
Of geraniums (red) and delphiniums (blue).

— From *When We Were Very Young*
A. A. Milne

Alan's poems were put in a
magazine. Then they were
published as a book. It was
called *When We Were Very*
Young. An artist named
E. H. Shepard drew pictures
for the poems.

Everyone wanted Alan to
write more poems for children.

Writing for Christopher Robin made Alan Milne
famous. Children around the world fell in love
with Winnie-the-Pooh and his forest friends.

34

Pen and ink illustration, by E. H. Shepard, shows Christopher Robin watching Pooh use an umbrella for a boat.

So for Christmas 1925, Alan wrote a bedtime story for Christopher. It was about Christopher's stuffed bear — Winnie-the-Pooh — and other toy animals in the nursery

*Illustration by
E. H. Shepard,
from the book*
Winnie-the-Pooh

that Christopher Robin
had named. There was
Eeyore (a donkey), Piglet
(a pig), Kanga (a mother
kangaroo), and Roo (Kanga's
little baby). Alan made up
two other characters for the
story — Owl and Rabbit.

Alan sent the story to a
newspaper, and it was
printed. Two years later,
it became a book called
Winnie-the-Pooh. E. H.
Shepard drew the pictures
for this book, too. He went
to the Milnes' country home to
draw Christopher and his toys.

*Pooh Bear chats with Christopher Robin outside
his house in the trunk of a tree.*
–Illustration by E. H. Shepard

Chapter 5

Always Something Going On

Alan wrote another book of
poems for children, called *Now
We Are Six*. It came out in 1927.
Here is one of the poems:

So wherever I am, there's always Pooh,
There's always Pooh and Me.
"What would I do?" I said to Pooh,
"If it wasn't for you," and Pooh said: "True,
It isn't much fun for One, but Two
Can stick together," says Pooh, says he.
"That's how it is," says Pooh.

— "Us Two", from *Now We Are Six*
A. A. Milne

Christopher Robin and his favorite toy bear

In 1928, Alan Milne wrote
a fourth and final children's
book. It was called *The House
at Pooh Corner*.

Christopher Robin meets with his friends from the enchanted forest: Piglet, Eeyore, Rabbit, Pooh, Owl, Kanga, Roo, and Tigger, too.

–Illustration by E. H. Shepard

In this book, a new
character joined
Pooh's adventures —
Tigger (a tiger).

41

A. A. Milne in his country home at Hartfield, Sussex, England

In 1929, Alan's brother Ken died. Then Alan's writing for children died, too. He still wrote plays and books for adults. However, most people cared more about his children's books.

Christopher grew up and
moved away. He fought
in World War II. Later,
he got married and then
opened a bookstore.

Alan and Daphne retired
to their farm in Cotchford.

*Mr. & Mrs. Milne enjoyed tea together
every afternoon.*

A. A. Milne

A. A. Milne lives on in the wonderful characters he created. As he once said, ". . . the Forest will always be there . . . and anybody who is Friendly with Bears can find it."

Alan A. Milne wrote
many books and plays
until he died in 1952.

He will always be
remembered for his
Winnie-the-Pooh
adventures with the
wonderful animals
who became Pooh's
friends in the magical
forest called the
Hundred Acre Wood.

Important Dates

1882 January 18 — Born in London, England, to Sarah Maria and John Vine Milne

1888 Began school at Henley House, London

1893 Entered Westminster School, London

1900 Entered Trinity College, Cambridge University

1906 Became assistant editor of *Punch* magazine

1913 Married Dorothy de Selincourt (Daphne)

1920 Christopher Robin born

1924 *When We Were Very Young* published

1926 *Winnie-the-Pooh* published

1927 *Now We Are Six* published

1928 *The House at Pooh Corner* published

1956 January 31 — Died at Cotchford Farm, near Hartfield, Sussex, England

Index

Page numbers in boldface type indicate illustrations.

PHOTO CREDITS

The Bettmann Archive—22, 23, 35, 36, 37, 40-41, 44 (bottom)
Hulton Deutsch—2, 10, 12-13, 14, 42, 43
Mary Evans Picture Library—44 (top); "Spy Junior", 24; Gunning King in
   Bibby's Annual (1910), 27
North Wind Picture Archives—4, 8, 20
SuperStock International, Inc.—National Portrait Gallery, 39
Tony Stone Images—© Mike Caldwell, 32
UPI/Bettmann Newsphotos—19, 29, 30, 34
Valan—© A. B. Joyce, 17
Cover illustration—Steven Gaston Dobson

ADDITIONAL CREDITS

Poem on page 33, "The Dormouse and the Doctor", from *When We Were Very Young* by A. A. Milne, Illustrations by E. H. Shepard. Copyright 1924 by E. P. Dutton, renewed 1952 by A. A. Milne. Used by permission of Dutton Children's Books, a division of Penguin Books USA Inc.

Poem on page 38, "Us Two", from *Now We Are Six* by A. A. Milne, illustrations by E. H. Shepard. Copyright 1927 by E. P. Dutton, renewed © 1955 by A. A. Milne. Used by permission of Dutton Children's Books, a division of Penguin Books USA Inc.

ANDERSON ELEMENTARY SCHOOL

105175001   921 MIL
A. A. Milne, author of...